Denys Parsons was educated at Eton and the universities of Munich and London. He has been a research chemist, educational and industrial film-maker and a group manager at the National Research Development Corporation. From 1973 to 1980 he was head of press and public relations at the British Library. He now combines a flourishing piano tuning business with writing and translating and editing for technical translation bureaux.

He started collecting funny misprints as a school-boy and his first book of them was published by Macdonald in 1952 after rejection by 12 other publishers. His major work was the *Directory of Tunes*, published in 1975. Denys Parsons is married with two sons and lives in north London.

Funnier By Far

DENYS PARSONS

Futura

A Futura Book

Copyright © Denys Parsons 1989

First published in Great Britain in 1989
by Futura Publications, a Division of
Macdonald & Co (Publishers) Ltd
London & Sydney

ISBN 0 7088 4323 9

Typeset in Baskerville by Fleet Graphics, Enfield, Middx

Reproduced, printed and bound in Great Britain by
BPCC Hazell Books Ltd
Member of BPCC Ltd
Aylesbury, Bucks, England

Futura Publications
A Division of
Macdonald & Co (Publishers) Ltd
66-73 Shoe Lane
London EC4P 4AB

A member of Maxwell Pergamon Publishing Corporation plc

INTRODUCTION

For those who have followed the exploits of Gobfrey Shrdlu since his first appearance in 1952, as chronicled in my fourteen books, there need be no introduction. For new readers I must explain that Shrdlu is the mischievous spirit who, I believe, lurks at the elbow of tired journalists and compositors, causing them to make these hilarious blunders. I took the name SHRDLU from Fleet Street; it is the counterpart on the printing machine of QWERTY on the typewriter.

Many of the items in this fifteenth Shrdlu book first appeared in *Punch* and *New Yorker*; others were contributed by fans – keen shrdlologists, I call them – and my particular thanks go to Patrick Moore, the astronomer, and Mary Pearce of Iver, Bucks.

So now read on, and split your sides laughing at Shrdlu's disastrous antics.

Motorway patrols reported severe congestion for two hours. The lorry was slightly injured and was taken to Chesterfield Royal Hospital for treatment.

Derby Evening Telegraph

Laura Charles is a physiotherapist who teached English to two others in her spare time.

Bradford Telegraph and Argus

Lady H—— was keen on the breed, having good sloping shoulders, strong hind quarters and hocks well let down.

Scottish Field

A man who stole a ballcock from an Abergavenny public toilet did so 'because the Almighty had told him it was to be done,' the town's magistrates heard. But when asked what he was going to do with it, he said he did not know because God had not told him.

Abergavenny Chronicle

Person between 23-30 years of age with education that includes HNC/HND or IWM required as Production Control Manager. Starting salary: min. £3,300 plus cat.

Current vacancies list

They would all have enjoyed UTV's movie on Tuesday, *The Body Snatchers*, which starred George Saunders and was made, I think, before he died.

Belfast Telegraph

ESSEX – First innings
Denness c Roebuck b Breakwell 39
East not out 63
McEwan not wanted 29

Leicester Mercury

A Padiham man who dived head first onto the sands at Blackpool was told by magistrates at the resort to go back home and try to straighten himself out.

Lancashire Evening Telegraph

Mr A.R. Cade, counsel for Thompson, said that although the facts were 'horrific', the cutting of the body in two pieces was 'only because it would not fit into the boot of the Morris Minor' – not to avoid detection.

Sydney Morning Herald

Mr Arthur Roberts, the council's principal engineer, said: 'There will also be ghost markings on the road to provide right turns into the cemetery.'

Watford Evening Echo

Jake was also worried by heavy coal wagons which regularly thundered past. He immediately called his dog Pepa, who also happens to be his wife, into the kerb.

Huddersfield District Examiner

When his woman friend suddenly walked out on him, a man kicked in the glass door of a Tiverton newsagents' shop and then went home and turned upside down.

Tiverton Gazette

VAN DRIVER required. Male/Female, over 21, up to 3 tons unladen weight.

Brighton Evening Argus

Dear Tourist,
Welcome to Jordan, the Holy Land, the loud of freasures and pleasures. We present to you this Touvist Gvide to help facilitate your stoy unorg as and we are glad to tell you how happy we are in your presence. please do not hesitate contact as on our address for in forwatin that are rot in cinded in this Guide. You con ever wrote to as for nore aiformation of veeded. We hope you a happy stoy ceveneng happy people. Again, welcome to Jordan.

Jordan This Week

The Santa Monica tenant, Bob Lewis, an actual local tenant, also served as a juror but he said he would 'be impartial and then vote to hang her.'

Ocean Front Weekly

A man caught trying to take away a car had a suspicious bulge under his shirt, Inspector Walters told Kidderminster magistrates.

Wolverhampton Express and Star

A partially blind man who was fined for drinking and driving swore this week he would never drive again. 'I can drive all right . . . I just can't see,' Mr Denton said.

Australasian Express

The thieves broke in in broad daylight on Bank Holiday Monday afternoon, eating through a louvre window.

Bournemouth Evening Echo

Tomorrow week the Canadian regimental doctors will be deposited for safe keeping in Bristol cathedral.

Bristol paper

Policeman Leo Grant was shot through the stomach and John Marden, taxi driver, through the hip, while a trusty at the jail was shot in the excitement.

San Francisco Call-Bulletin

FUNERALS
Parking for clients only

Notice at Surrey undertakers

Miss Y——, the well-known singer, was nearly poisoned at one time. So she said at the meeting on Tuesday. When she said she had been nearly poisoned, the features of the members expressed regret.

Irish paper

He's the same type as his son – forceful, aggressive, wanting to do things and get things done and above all, anxious to sin.

North Western Evening Mail

Although every possible care has been taken, I do not accept responsibility for inoccurancies.

Malta guidebook

The zoo will be open this week unless wildcat strike resumes.

Philadelphia Inquirer

The slow movement was beautifully managed and the finale taken briskly but with great rhythmic control and with plenty of time for the subtitles which abound in the movement.

Bristol paper

Meetings everywhere are crowded out. Not only that but luke-warm sympathisers are burning red-hot enthusiasts.

Clarion

First check the tyres for cuts and blemishes. Now get down on your knees, move them backwards and forwards, and if there is any appreciable shake, that indicates worn bearings or swivel pins.

Motor Mart

The dog was seen swimming around unable to get out of the water at Brierly Hill. The police were old and they asked the fire brigade for help.

Wolverhampton Express and Star

TO LET FURNISHED: self-contained flatlet. £30 per calendar month; hot water, lighting, rats inclusive.

Liverpool Echo

 **All staff must leave the building by the appointed fire exits, in an orderly manner (unless individually instructed otherwise).**

Fire Drill instruction

12

WANTED:
man to wash dishes and two waitresses

Notice in Sydney restaurant

13

Ladies! We are looking for cafeteria assistants to work in our modern cafeteria in the Grive Road area. Successful applicants will be asked to work occasionally.

South Wales Argus

Mr and Mrs John Gray are rejoicing over an eight-pound daughter, their sixth child since last Saturday.

Illinois paper

Some 13,500 other American citizens are now playing nursemaid to these South American rodents, envisioning wealth beyond the dreams of Ava Rice.

Pittsburgh Press

On making enquiries at the Hospital this after-noon, we learn that the deceased is as well as can be expected.

Jersey Evening Post

10.20 NEWS: WEATHERMAN
10.35 Beethoven's Erotica Symphony

Wishaw Press and Advertiser

Vauxhall lost £59,887,000 in the first six months. Compares with large carving knife still in her back. Neighbours heard that net loss of £7m in first half of last year.

Swindon Evening Advertiser

St Andrew's Church forms an elegant background to excavations for the main sewer in Cheltenham.

Gloucestershire Echo

The Society of Government Meeting Planners held its inaugural meeting recently to discuss the problems of meeting planning and plan its next meeting on planning meetings.

Washington Post

There, the 140-ton crane will be waiting to unload the boilers onto steel rollers. The boilers will be pulled into the plant by a wench.

Pittsburgh Press

The doctor smiled reassuringly at the worried mother and patted her little bot on the cheek.

From a paperback book

Many housewives can't even tell storks from butter, according to TV advertisements in Britain.

South China Morning Post

For a few hours there was confusion in Washington, as President Reagan lay under the surgeon's wife.

Turkish Daily News

> *Customers not collecting their shoe repairs within six months will be disposed of.*

Notice in Bognor shop

The operation to trap the gang began on Friday when a man arrived from Morocco on a car ferry. His car was followed to Prestwick where police ponced.

The Guardian

PARK ENDS SPRAYING
DUTCH FOR ELM DISEASE

Grosse Pointe News, Michigan

The procession was very fine, and nearly two miles in length, as was also the sermon of the minister.

New York Times

What Mrs Thatcher's closest friends are wondering is whether, as the signs suggest, she is beginning to suffer from metal fatigue.

The Guardian

Literarcy week observed

Brandenburg Messenger, Kentucky

Stop Press: British Rail has announced it cannot guarantee Southern region services, so things are returning to normal.

The Independent

NEW ORLEANS – Baseball people get up yesterday to read the local paper and see that the Mets dealt Rusty Staub to the Phillies. Of course, the writer had heard it from know that the deal had know that the deal had another writer an didn't fallen through. Anyway, he had the principles mixed up.

Boston Globe

Winners in the home-made claret section were Mrs Davis (fruity, well-rounded), Mrs Rayner (fine colour and full-bodied), and Miss Smith (slightly acid, but should improve if laid down).

From a Leicester parish magazine

Jack was born on Sunday, February 15, after having rushed his father from a nearby tennis court and his mother to hospital only 45 minutes before being born.

Kensington & Chelsea Times

The Italian doctor looked at me fixedly above his plate of ravioli and tomato and his smile displayed thirty-two artistically-aligned molars.

Touring-Club

Widower wishes to correspond with lady of 60 to 68 years old with a view to marriage and able to milk a cow.

Echo Républicain de la Beaune

Madame Quillet's assassin, after striking her, had strangled his victim with blows from a hatchet.

Parisien Libéré

I like to be completely independent and feel the only way I can be is to love away from home.

Glasgow Evening Times

Make your suite reservations now and with our confirmation we will send you a voucher for free dinner for two on your honeymoon (good for one night only).

Advert for Niagara Falls Hotel

Another hazard is weed killer. If wild growth on road verges looks yellow and dying at a time when it should be flourishing, the council have probably been praying there.

Dog World

Warmest welcome was reserved for Mrs Muriel Wood, 55, who has tried for nearly 30 years to get women admitted. Crowds of men gathered round her, shook her head and said, 'Well done, Muriel.'

Daily Mail

FOR SALE: Antique dog basket with 3-kw electric blow heater and log effect, £30.

ABC Weekly Advertiser

Miss Janeston, known as 'the Bird Woman of Ainger Road' was jailed for a week because she refused to stop feeding Judge Donald Morganson at Liverpool.

Evening Herald, Dublin

There were only eight days during February without sin, the longest period being 7.5 hours on 4 February.

Rhyl and Prestatyn Gazette

When a South Shields man was found in a car he admitted using keys to get into it, and taking off his socks so that he would not leave fingerprints.

Shields Gazette

At the request of the dog catcher, the Council has debated whether or not to employ him on a demand basis. They have also discussed appointing a dog.

Evening Chronicle, Newcastle

Southern Television programme change.

Delete *Husband of the Year* and insert *Dogsbody*

Agency announcement

Life in the Isle of Wight was hard with a severe shortage of food. The winter of 1944 was the worst, with no gas, electricity or coal Mrs N. Jackson was pianist and refreshments were served.

Isle of Wight Weekly Post

Please note – Money, defined below, may be sent by the Compensation Fee Parcel service, but no compensation will be payable in the event of loss or damage.

Post Office information leaflet

City police are worried that 68 rifles and shotguns stolen from a city warehouse may end up in the hands of criminals.

Edmonton Journal

Plain woolly gloves look drab in evening outings but few of us can afford the kid or suede alternative at today's prices. A quick and easy way to brighten them up is to buy a beetroot over and then mix with some horseradish cream.

Eltham Times

The wife of the council's chairman of Northants County Council, worth £3,000, was stolen from their home last week and has not been recovered.

Bedfordshire on Sunday

At the January meeting Mrs Mary Nelson entertained members with a show of slides covering a visit to Australia, various beauty spots and views of Seil, finishing with slides showing the variety of things to see in outer space.

Oban Times

Ambulancemen grabbed the arm of a young man as he was about to jump six floors from the top of the *Sunday Times* building in Grays Inn Road, and hauled him to safety. 'We offered him a cup of tea but he said he wasn't falling for that.'

Evening News

James was bitten by a spider on the head while on holiday with his parents at Wamleral, near Gosford on the Central Coast. The spider, believed to be in a track suit, bit the boy while he was dressing.

New South Wales Daily Mirror

Yesterday Mr Jenkins remarked that Mr Robinson didn't have the brains of an idiot and, when asked to withdraw the observation said this would amount to a declaration that Mr Robinson did have the brains of an idiot.

Rand Daily Mail

The open grave has been filled in, and the contents replaced by the Vicar and his curate, the Revd. Simon Carter.

Yorkshire Post

Energy is the foundation upon which ever more complex societies are laid and sustained. Energy is the glue that keeps things apart.

Idaho paper

'DON'T PRINT THE STORY OF MY TRIAL,' SHE SOBS

Full amazing story – page 10.

Sunday Mail, Scotland

Mrs Elizabeth Smith (Chairman) gave a talk on Spain, including a description of a bullfight at the luncheon meeting of Cowplain and Waterlooville Ladies Club.

Portsmouth and Southsea Evening News

Mikhelson said in an interview this month that archaeologists might have been usable for such a project if they had not been put into strong formaldehyde preservatives by their discoverers.

Michigan Daily

However, my mother is strongly against the idea of wearing contact lenses and has found out that they may not be suitable for everyone. Can any obstetrician enlighten me on this matter?

Straits Times

Three old men sat ˙on the wench, munching sandwiches.

Weekly News, New Zealand

Deaf viewers with the special decoding device will see the picture with the captions; to others the TV picture will appear exactly as it does not.

Boston Globe

Lady requires work for 6 hours per week to clean small officers at Station Road, Witney.

Witney and West Oxfordshire Gazette

Application forms and £1,925 may be obtained from the County Librarian, County Hall

Evening Argus, Brighton

A traffic signal at the main entrance to Greenwood Hall Road was recently changed to a flashing signal Road was recently changed to a flashing signal Road was recently changed to a flashing signal because of an electrical malfunction.

Bowling Green Park Daily News, Kentucky

I have had many complaints of dogs running free and have bitten several people in South Riverwoods.

Riverwoods Newsletter, Illinois

The service was conducted by the Revd Peter S———. After the Benedictine, Mr and Mrs Taylor sang 'I'll walk beside you.'

Report of wedding

Mrs A. P. Payne will not be at home today, owing to her absence from home.

Brisbane Courier

A strong link between the records of fathers and their sins has been discovered by two researchers.

New York Daily News

Will the individual who borrowed a ladder from the caretaker last month kindly return same immediately, otherwise further steps will be taken.

Notice in Leicestershire village

Instant hot water
in five minutes

Notice in York boarding house

The bridesmaids, both sisters of the bride, wore dresses of lavender and blue net respectively, with head-dresses and mittens to tone. Both carried Victorian Derek Bates brother of the bridegroom.

Penrith Observer

ARMY OFFICER FIRES TOY PISTOL

Fined for dangerous driving

Khartoum Morning News

The coffee house will have the services of two efficient 'captains' and twelve polite and courteous waitresses, specially selected for their experiences, to attend to customers.

Straits Times

FOR SALE, Three-piece suite.
Settee turns into bed covered in
thick yellow mustard.

Advert in local paper

Turreted, arched and almost unbearably picturesque, you can walk round them unresented.

Evening Standard

The Trade Secretary confirmed that the five British Airways Concordes had developed cracks in reply to a written question from a Labour MP.

Financial Times

'Concerto for two trumpets in C' by Vivaldi will feature Michael and Robbert Diggins, who are violinists in the orchestra.

A Los Angeles college journal

The commission says R—— initially tried to justify the report, but when its inconsistencies with available facts were pointed out to him he burst into tears and, like a lanced boil, made a clean breast of it.

Financial Times

Even Scott of the Antarctic would have been daunted waiting for a bus in Halesowen, councillors heard. For in an impassioned plea for more shelters to help bus travellers bear the cold, Coun. Brown told them: 'If Captain Scott had visited here he would never have bothered going to the South Pole.'

Worcester Evening News

After the accident patrolman William De Haven took up the chase after the Harding auto, noting that Harding was riding on the rim of the right front tire.

Ardmore Times, Pennsylvania

Mrs Carter says she knows of six cats which have disappeared after reading a national newspaper story highlighting pet skins being exported to Germany.

Comet, Letchworth

Mushrooms Provençale stuffed with the Chef's special recipe and friend in garlic butter.

Blackburn Citizen

What is a reasonable time laid down by the Post Office top brass for waiting for service? Mr D. White, Assistant Postmaster for the area, came up with the answer: 'Under normal conditions any person waiting in excess of five minutes is abnormal. We wouldn't be happy with a person waiting longer than that.'

Review on Sunday, St Albans

LOST, One pair lady's navy blue suede sandals, size 8, assumed dropped in gents toilet at the Recovery Home in West Street.

Leicester Mercury

The shootout took place at Holford Place after the dead man had contacted the police and arranged to give himself up.

Perth Sunday Times

The possibility of necrophiliacs working in the cemeteries, paedophiles in the playground, and even heterosexuals mixing with people of the opposite sex occupied the minds of Waltham Forest councillors last week.

Waltham Forest Guardian

FOR SALE. One Large Headmaster, answers to name Jock, housetrained, £10 or near offer.

Merseymart

DRESS SHOPS. Even Lady Diana would look good in one of our range of dresses.

Advert in Sutton Coldfield News

Jim Williams – now occupying the key post of party vice-chairman (policy) – swayed the conference with his oratory. There was a roar of applause when he declared: Turn to Page 12.

Scots Independent

The report examines the proposed closure of the Centre by the DHSS in four years time. 'What homeless single people have in common,' says the report, 'is that they are single and homeless.'

London Housing

SIDCUP – A most attractive house (re-built 1948) in excell dec condition, sit in a most sought after posn on the Sidcup—New Eltham borders. New Eltham Stn is within easy reach providing a very good service to the City and bathrm.

Kentish Independent

We assure fluency in English in two months. British School of Language. Method: Microwave.

Advert in Times of India

To those of you who think that the RNLI National Lottery is always won by someone else, take heart. The £250 prize in the twelfth draw was won by Mrs M.K. Stanhope of Leigh-on-Sea.

Yachting Monthly

WEST BERLIN: Horse Beck, 36, an hotel porter, was jailed for 18 months by a West Berlin Court. He had been searching wastepaper baskets for East German security agents.

Daily Mail

A seventeen-year-old Copnor youth was remanded in custody to Portsmouth Quarter Sessions by Portsmouth Magistrates yesterday after he admitted stealing three bicycles, a record player, thirty-one records, a National Insurance Card, and two cases of false pretences.

Portsmouth Evening News

Unaccompanied ladies not admitted unless with husband or similar.

Notice in Cairo bar

The raiders took about £600 in cash. 'They left nothing untouched, the whole place was a shabgm' selM'bolaletaoin a shambles,' Mr Higgins said.

North Berks Herald

A fisherman who returned home to find his wife in bed with a foreign fisherman had been under the impression that she had been paying the rates, magistrates at Louth heard on Thursday.

Louth Leader

On the following day, Paul Roberts will perform 'Perambulation for Violin' and 'Sonata for Violin, Piano and Two Tomato Sandwiches.'

North West Artful Reporter

His Passionate Love (USSR). A film about the problem of production management which is very acute today.

Moscow News

A woman arrested as a prostitute claimed that she was too short-sighted to ply for trade. Mrs Mary Palmer, 48, said she was blind in one eye and vision in the other was blurred. She told Southend magistrates: 'I can only see if someone is right on top of me.'

Southend Evening Echo

BABY alive in box plus four sets of clothes excellent condition, £11 the lot.

Yorks and District Advertiser

Something different in musical programming. An interesting blend of contemporary music, jazz and Newfoundland folksongs performed by filthy leading Newfoundland musicians.

Newfoundland TV Topics

Police are looking for a missing estate of 110 houses, complete with roads, lamp standards and trees.

Yorkshire Post

Menus in the Commons dining room will be printed in English and not French in future. Potages and consommés become soup and chips so all MPs can understand.

Southend Evening Echo

An MP has called on the Government to provide more protection for mothers-in-law against scorpions.

Luton Post-Echo

The do-it-yourself plumber from Lytham, wrapped only in a towel, was attacked by his pet kitten as he bent down and was knocked unconscious by hitting his head on the sink, and then received a broken arm as he was accidentally tipped off a stretcher by an ambulanceman who could not stop laughing.

Lancashire Evening Post

When the so-called Great Education Debate moved to Dorset, some employers criticised the standards of reding, speeling and pungtuation of school leavers.

Bournemouth Evening Echo

'We'd love to have more litter bins,' he told me, 'but it's not the expense. It's just the fact that they are misused. People put parcels of rubbish into them.'

Edinburgh Evening News

The Green family have played an important part in the life of Steeton. Mr Don Green was the owner of a textile mill in Steeton and a well-known former Girl Guide.

Bradford Telegraph and Argus

Barnfield said the research and development and high technology aspects of the Energy Deparergy decision making ion, a consumer group. 'This will make energy decision making ion, a consumer group. 'This will make energy decision making ion, a consumer group. 'This will make energy decision making ion, a consumer group. 'This will make energy decision making more confusimer group. 'This will make energy decision making more confusing at oup. 'This will make energy decision making more confusing at a time when we desperately need to have an organised focus on the program.'

Greenwich Time, USA

 **CREMATION FACTS ON**

1. Immediate Cremation
2. Conventional Cremation
3. Do-It-Yourself

Advert in Burlington Vanguard Press, Vermont

The test is simple and consists of holding one's breath for twenty-five minutes.

Our Town

Before you're allowed to give blood, Wright says, you have to fill out a questionnaire on your medical background – 33 questions on everything from are you running a fever to have you ever had a social disease. 'All 33 answers have to be yeses,' Wright says. 'Only then are you eligible to donate blood.'

News-Star-World, Louisiana

All suspects picked out by witnesses from police records have been questioned and eliminated from the inquiry. Scores of motor-cycles have also been interviewed with, so far, negative results.

Athens News

The bride, who was given away by her father, wore a dress of white figured brocade with a trailing veil held in place by a coronet of pearls. She carried a bouquet of rose buds and goods vehicles, leaving free access to all private vehicles not built for more than seven passengers.

Atherstone News and Herald

Sprinkle on the shelves a mixture of half borax and half sugar. This will poison every aunt that finds it.

Norwick Bulletin, Connecticut

Bats have fallen prey to pesticides, and the felling of dead trees has caused so many of their usual habitats being destroyed. A group of conservation volunteers showed visitors how to build a bat roasting box.

Keynsham Weekly Chronicle

Among Saturday's highlights were a breathtaking display of sky diving by the Northern Sky Divers, which included 28-year-old Mr Paul Wilson, and two horses and a number of obedient hounds from the Middleton Hunt.

Yorkshire Evening Press

Now in mint condition after being renovated by a cigarette manufacturing company in Harare, secretary Miss Melissa Skyum (22) tried her hand at working the museum piece.

Zimbabwe Herald

If it had not been for the United States Navy, the World War would have resulted in the real Agamemnon that so many predicted at the time.

U.S. Naval Air Station bulletin

The husband's allegation of cruelty was rejected, but the judge exercised discretion in respect of his own misconduct.

Daily Mail

'We do not want a repetition of the farce that occurred on the last occasion we saw the Board,' he said, 'when a lot of sand was thrown in our eyes. This time we want something more concrete.'

Fulham Chronicle

NOTICE

Any persons passing beyond this point will be drowned

BY ORDER OF THE MAGISTRATES

Sign in Essex village

His other preoccupation will be weaving, a pastime he has developed during his long walks.

Yorkshire Post

In addition, the seminars are being handled as a major media event by the Government, which is concerned that the public believe it is thinking.

Toronto Globe and Mail

This Sunday only, children are invited to participate in a dog contest at 2 p.m. The dogs will be judges on beauty, health and intelligence.

Montreal Gazette

News from the hospitals:
Admitted: Gay Tufarolo, 107 Main Street.
Discouraged: Mrs Elizabeth Cook, Holly Hill.

Daytona Beach Evening News

The fox made a bee-line through the Hall grounds, then on through the village, to the delight of the hundreds of spectators. A few moments later there were shouts in a garden near to the church, and within a few minutes the hounds had killed these scores of sightseers looking on from the surrounding gardens. It was one of the most exciting days we can remember.

Wilts paper

CARLISLE's one-way traffic experiment, which brought vehicles in the city centre to a halt yesterday morning, achieved its object, claimed Mr L.A. Harris, the City surveyor and engineer.

Northern paper

The bride and bridegroom left for Italy, the latter wearing a hyacinth-blue hat of crinoline straw, and a blue velvet cloak over a dress of hyacinth-blue crêpe de Chine.

Essex paper

If the motion were passed, no strike action would be taken by NALGO without a ballet of all its members.

Bristol Evening Post

There have been times when I used to follow a lonely white-eye in the forest singing lustily all the time, hopping from tree to tree, as though calling for a mate.

Daily Mail

Coun. Barker told them: 'The red herring of car parking has gone back and forwards until it has become a bogeyman.'

Westmoreland Gazette

16 Dane Road, Cheam – erection of a two-storey extension, a first-floor rear extension and formation of a pitched roof over part of Mr D. Barnes.

Sutton Herald

A sprinkling of local entrants are included in the list of more than 6,000 competitors and yesterday sheep farmers from the Huddersfield area were among the prizes.

Huddersfield Daily Examiner

They make all these emotive allegations, but when you nail them down they don't stand up.

West Sussex County Times

The expert also said that, in the traditional Westminster system, an MP would be able to cross the floor without vacating his seat.

Rhodesia Herald

The sudden fierce gust of wind took all who were at the ceremony completely by surprise. Hats were blown off and copies of the Vicar's speech and other rubbish were scattered over the site.

Ninfield and Hooe Parish News

Experiment began in disaster when Malcolm Pringle played back to a ball of good length from Bill Croft, failed to cover and caught woodworm.

Yorkshire Evening Press

Experienced Secretary. Aged 24, well educated and with excellent qualifications seeks interesting and gearbox with varnished hardwood body . . . No HGV, very easy to drive. Bargain £1,950, plus VAT.

Horse and Hound

Apparently three girls in very brief bikinis turned up at the airport to greet the Prince of Wales and someone had them removed.

The Australian

If you are buried on a weekday, notify the Town Manager's Office by 10 a.m. the day before. If you are buried on the weekend, notify the Town Manager's Office by 10 a.m. on the last regular workday prior to the day of interment.

Culpeper News

There is no housing shortage. It is a wicked lie put out to discredit the government by people who have nowhere to live.

Hindustan Times

The talk on leather accessories was given by Mrs Jean Hayes, who showed a varied selection of her work, including her skilled love-making, and she was thanked by Mrs Laura Field.

East Kent Gazette

Maurienne is a beautiful area. Although the Arc Valley is an industrial area the slopes of Maurienne remain a prolific garden. Maurienne is also the birthplace of Jean Jacques Rousseau, the famous underwater explorer.

South Africa Family Radio & TV

THETFORD FIRM GIVES KIDNEY SUFFERERS NEW HEART

East Anglian Daily Times

Mr Long and Bud Moore went deer hunting and shot a deer at Jonesboro. Also their guest, Alan Hancock, from Ashland, Maine.

News Observer, Maine

Terrine of hare: Completely de-bone a hare. Remove all the flesh. Put aside the wings which you can soak in brandy for 24 hours.

Le Pèlerin

Boat for sale, one owner, green in colour.

Card in shop window

Embarkation and disembarkation: passenger taxes,

Passengers of all classes: nil
Steerage passengers   : nil

These taxes will be halved for passengers to and from Cameroun.

French travel leaflet

A Paris police superintendent was yesterday trying to decide whether a portion of cream cheese constitutes a dangerous police car.

Daily Telegraph

Dennis Harris, playing solo trumpet in the Bedford Band was awarded the medal for the best trombone player in the section.

Leigh Journal

Mid-Cheshire Central College
of Further Education

A MALE CLEANER BSc(Eng), C Eng, FIMechE, MIProdE is required for the Main College at Hartford.

Advert in Northwich Chronicle

**Please carry dog
or hang on the hook
on the wall.**

Notice in Bristol shop

1979 Hillman Hunter. Auto saloon. One owner. God. Nominal mileage.

Advert in Biggleswade Chronicle

The stampede occued when the cush of people on the staiway ushed to get the taditional ice cakes thown by a piest, boke down a nine-foot guad wall, mingled with sceaming falling people. Police said that about 40,000 people wee at the shine. – Reute

Liverpool Daily Post

A Felling man who almost strangled his estranged wife to death was given a second chance by the judge.

Gateshead Post

A very useful service is offered by GARDEN CULTIVATION LTD. They will turn a garden into a wilderness under the expert supervision of Mr David French.

Evening Gazette, Middlesborough

A man we know also saw the strange figure and it upset him so much that he has not eaten property for some days.

Sheffield Star

Gunalan was deadly on his smashes from the back of the court and kept Ghosh guessing by mixing in some delightful drop shorts.

Anrita Bazar Patrika, Calcutta

BIG PETWORTH WIN FOR QUEEN

Major show success for Windsor cow

The News, Portsmouth

BRIDES-TO-BE. Your trousseau require 12-bore L.Franchi shotgun, over and under, as new, $360.

AUSTIN 1100, 24,000 miles, service certificate, lady under radio, extras, £485.

Prior to his return to work this morning he spent the weekend at his fiancée's home and is now back on the job better versed in business methods.

Negro singer Gereros Dorsetta has refused to give any evidence to New York police about the night-club shooting which resulted in Billy Daniels, the coloured singer, being charged with assault and carrying a gnu.

Alderman M. Barrett: 'There you have a classic example of how by question and answer an innuendo is freely displayed in the Council Chamber, blown sky-high, and brought back as a boomerang on the people who tried to set it alight.'

The bait has been a new generation of £80,000 luxury coaches, with air suspension, free video films, a built-in toilet with coffee and sandwiches served at one's seat.

Yorkshire Post

Fauré: Requiem, and Walton: Miss A. Brevis. The Carlyon Singers at St Michael's Church, Newquay.

Cornish Guardian

Schoolboy Robert Welsh, aged ten, had a lucky escape early today his hay fever caught fire spreading flames which damaged the bed and bedroom carpet.

Bristol Evening Post

Still, when one looks at how this government have cooked the unemployment figures the sky is the limit to how low they can descend.

The Scotsman

Mr and Mrs Robert Parker have much pleasure in announcing the engagement of their daughter, Cynthia to Ken, son of Mrs good cond., works well. $50 Edna Finch.

Sydney Morning Herald

SOLOIST at the Trinity Y.P.U. meeting referred to on Saturday, Miss McKenzie sang the solo, Lord Speak To Me, not Miss McDonald.

Canadian paper

Driver David Markham avoided any bumps in the road and took the corners slowly as he delivered a baby girl.

Southern Evening Echo

Israeli jets last night launched a three hour attack on an old people's home in Torquay.

Hereford Evening News

Harper might easily have killed his nephew and people had got to learn that the use of knives, even on relatives, would not be tolerated.

Richmond and Twickenham Times

Miss Grant has NO male goat this season, and refers all clients to Mr Harris.

Advert in Grantham Journal

Granting a decree to a wife at Swansea Assizes, Mr Commissioner Johnson said her husband wrote her a letter which should not have been sent to a dog.

News of the World

In the end the weather was I can't read this word but the water smoother than expected.

Monmouthshire Free Press

He said that speeds of over 100 m.p.h. were reached in the police chase which followed, until the stolen cat crashed in Bowring Park, Liverpool.

Southport Midweek Visiter

Kuala Lumpur – City Hall today announced the closure of Jalan Sungai Besi to facilitate repair work on the overhead pedestrian bridge which is to be demolished.

New Straits Times

EAR PIERCING £1.99 including studs.
Digital batteries fitted.

Advert in Brighton and Hove Leader

Keith came into prominence when he won the world title in January, but it took him eight years to become an overnight sensation.

Dundee Sporting Post

But after his death last year, Mr Hugh S——, a tough Right-winger, recaptured the seat for Labour, surviving two recounts to emerge winner by 289 votes.

Yorkshire Post

The figure was nearer 50 per cent for the Port Augusta Jail and nearly all female prisoners in Port Augusta were female, said Mr Stanley.

Weekend Australian

The mortuary will be built despite stiff opposition.

Surrey and Kingston Guardian

Sister Barham of the Holy Family Convent, London, met the Pope at a private audience because she uses a Gestetner duplicator.

Glasgow Evening Times

No matter which service a new recruit enters now, if he is going to be a cook he goes to one centre, if he is going to drive heavy vehicles he is sent to another, and if he is going to be a police dog he goes to a third.

Classical Music

An Oxford cyclist who was knocked over by a bus is the first major success in a Friends of the Earth scheme.

Oxford Star

WANTED, rocking horse, suit 3-year-old (unemployed) reasonable price.

Advert in Lancaster Guardian

Mr Robert Farr, chairman of a Wellington advertising company involved in producing television commercials, said that advertisements may not reflect society exactly but they certainly mirror it.

Auckland Star

After the service the Salvation Army Band led the procession to the war memorial. Then as the congregation stood with heads bowed a lone burglar from the Welsh Guards played the Last Post.

Woking Informer

Next on the agenda is WNO's spell-binding production of Puccini's Bohème, featuring favourites like Rodolfo's 'Young Tiny Head is Frozen.'

Chipping Sodbury Gazette

For a dinner party in his flat for six guests recently he did melon in sparkling wine, French onion soup, chicken with port. Guests bought wine, the men wore Gruyère and Marsala, sorbet, cheese and dinner jackets as usual, the girls romantic frocks.

Northern Echo

A couple and their two children fought their way through smoke from a fire which started in the front room of their house in Ellora Road, Streatham. Fire-lighters extinguished the blaze.

Streatham News

Using careful combinations of spices and herbs the chef produces delicious dishes like Bengal Chicken, a medium hot dry curry which is succulently flavoured with micemeat.

Alton Post-Dispatch

It should be noted that the problem with the bed-wetting turned out to be due to a hole in the patient's water bed and not due to any problem with the patient himself.

Medical insurance report

When the motion was carried, the Mayor presented a gold medallion to the Retiring Mayor, and the Mayoress to the Retiring Mayoress.

Oldham Evening Chronicle

But the scheme may be dropped following a meeting between campaigners trying to rid the area of prostitutes, councillors and police.

Wandsworth Guardian

A motorist whose car clipped another vehicle passing on the other side of the road, causing slight damage, was found to have over three times the legal amount of alcohol in her briefs when she was eventually stopped.

Fulham Chronicle

A leek has closed the scenic Llangollen canal in North Wales only eight months after major repairs.

Wolverhampton Express and Star

The existing butchery block at St George's Hospital, Morpeth, is to be converted to a mortuary as part of a scheme to upgrade the main kitchens etc.

Morpeth Herald

Gallons of inflammable cellulose thinners and petroleum-based police had been sprinkled across both floors of the 20,000 sq. ft factory.

Islington Gazette

Mrs J. Gearing of Sebring, Florida, is visiting this week in the home of Mrs Melvina Burtis. Mrs Gearing died a few years ago.

Ludlow Tribune, Vermont

Mr Gumo said, however, that the introduction of speed trains would not be an immediate undertaking. 'With speed trains one would arrive at one's destination too early. At the present time you get to your destination just at the right time,' he added.

The Nation, Nairobi

Busts, which ceased to matter last season, seem to have disappeared altogether, except for evening when they pop rather startlingly above the neckline.

Evening Standard

An opportunity will shortly be available for a secretary of impeachable character, in a small office, of a new industry shortly opening near Redruth.

West Briton

Gentleman has several small houses let to tenants he wishes to dispose of.

Dalton's Weekly

Andrew Roberts and Thomas Green have been sentenced to periods of youth custody after failing to break a Lymington jeweller's window with a concrete slab.

Southern Evening Echo

He revealed: 'We arrested one woman with a whole salami in her knickers. When asked why, she said she was missing her Italian boyfriend.'

Manchester Evening News

The crowds have dwindled during the years but the Botanical Gardens remain as popular as ever.

Birmingham Evening Mail

The court was told that, after the attack, Parker had told a VicRail employee he was God. The employee had then asked for some identification.

Melbourne Sun

Princess Anne attended the opening in a stunningly bright peach-coloured kimono-like gown that fittingly suited the evening's Japanese tenor.

Leader-Post, Saskatchewan

Research scientist Rory Jack Thompson yesterday promised a jury that he would never again murder his wife as he did last year.

The West Australian

The ability to perform a perfect darn on a hole in a sock is a real skill which, unfortunately, is almost totally useless when it comes to replacing a pane of glass in the kitchen window.

Exeter Express and Echo

LONDON MARKED PLATES required, complete set. Exchange grandfather, or cash.

Exchange & Mart

NORTH SIDE, nice 4-bedroomed home, possession 15 days. Colonel Marker lived in this place 2 years and is in very good condition.

San Antonio News

In 1911 he worried Mrs Laura Little of Montgomery, Alabama. They have three children.

Philadelphia Inquirer

Motor vehicle safety belts must be installed rigidly enough to withstand a sudden thirst.

Trenton Times

Bathroom suite, Twyford Primrose, pedestal washbasin, close coupled symphonic w.c. with matching seat.

Hemel Hempstead Gazette

6.30 Divertimento.
7.30 Italian strings to Spanish reeds.
9.30 Mozart - Music for Basset Hounds.

Melbourne Age

The Merchant of Venice: One of Shakespeare's masterpieces famous for its great theatrical protagonist Shylock the Jew and his quest to find a husband for his beautiful daughter Portia.

Tourist magazine

If you contact our association from morning time to 12.30 a.m. give you a certain way to release the suffering from rheumatism, sore-bone and bumbness.

South China Morning Post

The Minister for Minerals and Energy, Mr Parker, plans to release the report and give people till mid-July to comment on it. The Government will then review the comments and fake a decision.

The West Australian

Radio Three: 10.15: Stereo Release (s). 11.15
BBC Sympathy Orchestra in Germany (s).

Hull Daily Mail

He told the bench that Bartram had to take anti-consultant drugs and tranquillisers.

Stevenage Comet

CHAMBERMAID
HAD POT

Brighton Evening Argus

When challenged and told he would be charged with fishing, X replied, 'So what?' He then threw a piece of bread at one of the officers, catching him in the temple. Had the bread been buttered it might have caused a nasty mark.

Bournemouth Evening Echo

Howard county planners are considering a proposal to prohibit more than three pets (dogs, cats, etc.) on any lot smaller than 3 acres. Mr Harris said, 'We don't want a definition of pets to include goldfish, for example, unless they are running round the yard unleashed.'

Baltimore Sun

As far as languages go, Tony Hart does give a word of warning: 'The new technique is no substitute for learning a language properly. Like all computers it is very litral and words have to be spelt out correctly.'

Manchester Evening News

Usually the information given in your magazine is concise and accurate, but your article on Circumcision (November) left certain points uncovered.

Letter in Mother Magazine

Attending the bride was Miss Sarah Collins who wore a peach silk gown with yolk insects of lace and frilled at the hemline with two small attendants who behaved impeccably throughout the service. Mr Jones was wearing a beige and navy dress and jacket with navy straw hat trimmed with white.

Isle of Man Courier

The most crowded wards are maternity and orthopaedic; 30 per cent of all admissions are the result of accident.

Medical Laboratory World

The Yorkshire Ripper, Mr George R——, has been ordered to take a 'complete rest'.

Western Morning News

The case had originally been heard at the end of August, but because a juror tried to tell a witness a joke about an octopus the judge ordered a retrial.

South London Press

A Seattle man who hijacked a plane demanded one million dollars in cash and a parachute. After six hours bargaining he changed his demand to three cheeseburgers.

Sunderland Echo

New Ideal Homes has an immediate vacancy for a Clerk/Typist. Competent typing and a pleasing telephone manner essential. We feel that the job might well suit a mature parson.

Woking News and Mail

CHILDREN IN SCHOOL LUNCH SANDWICH

Richmond Herald

Guyana is different from the other Caribbean islands because it is not an island. It is not even near the Caribbean sea.

Pakistan Star

The consultant diagnosed a congenial heart defect.

Bournemouth Evening Echo

The 42,000-ton *Vanguard* was the last of the great British battleships. The keel was laid in 1941, but she was not commissioned until 1946 and was destined never to fire massive 15-in. buns in battle.

Glasgow Evening Times

The ASTMS national officer told *Computing*: 'Our action is designed to close the company down, the purpose being to get the plant closure decision rescinded.'

Computing

Little Parndon Junior School held their Harvest Festival celebrations last week. They delivered 66 food parcels to the elderly residents living locally in a large box.

Harlow Gazette

Next week – Sunday November 4th – the topic will be 'Family Love'. Brochures illustrating the whore program are available at the entrance of the church.

A Quebec parish bulletin

Donors provided everything from a Twin Otter airplane to drop supplies at the remote polar base camp to chewing gum with which they will exercise their jaws while subsisting on mushy packaged rations. Several companies developed new technologies for them, including ropes that fasten with knots.

Denver Post

V Sinclair ZX81, factory made, complete, power supply, manuals (2), games cassette, as new, sell £100 or exchange concrete mixer.

Exchange & Mart

Singles Club. If you think that your social life couldn't possibly be any more boring than it already is, join the Ecclesall Twenties Club and we might prove you wrong!

Sheffield Star

Brown purse lost on bus by working woman; contains money, buttons, union card, sick husband.

San Francisco Examiner

Retired now from active mission work, he is 'doing the work of the Lord on the side' while following his earlier and more respectable trade as a boss bricklayer.

Washington Star

Wanted – Potential managers are required for City Bank. Persons between 25 and 30 with 40 years experience.

Lloyds Bank magazine

Asked by the magistrate why he spoke with an American accent when he was born and raised in South Africa and had never visited the United States, Mr Mason replied that he stayed with a white family who were Scottish.

Salisbury Herald

Lochgilphead Gaelic Choir are holding a Whist in the Royal Hotel, Ardrishaig on Wednesday, February 10 at 8 p.m. Admission 60p. (Light Supper will be survived.)

Argyllshire Advertiser

Although this telephone booth is unique, it is quite typical of many others in the country.

New Straits Times

Miss Ruth Mitchell was injured at the farm of her grandfather, Whitney Dean, Thursday by being ignored by a cow.

New York Times

Three of the bridesmaids wore plain cream dresses with blue print cotton panels while the small bridesmaid had a plain cream bodice with blue print skirt and frilled hem. They carried bouquets of cream carnations and cornflakes.

The Orcadian

Normans Bay level crossing will be closed to traffic for the next three weekends while railway engines repair the road.

Bexhill-on-Sea Observer

In the Doncaster district there are more underground cables than overhead, but this is largely due to Doncaster having its cables underground.

Yorkshire Evening Post

Like all papers written by people following an infinite end, the welter of have and have not, with regard to what may, if by any chance it ever, though it should, of course, is a little confusing.

Stockport Advertiser

An Australian Federal Police recruit was helped to his feet by fellow officers after fainting at a passing out parade.

Canberra Times

Mr John Parker believes the funeral processions could be involved in serious accidents on the fast stretch of the London Road. Mr Parker said: 'I am not at all happy with the access to and from the cemetery and i think it is a possible death trap.'

St Albans Midweek Advertiser

The night a fish and chip war broke out rival chipmen battered each other.

Luton Evening Post

A spokesman for the Stewardship Committee said this week that the two million lapel badges which were distributed bearing the message 'God loves a fiver' should have read 'God loves a giver'. The badges can be amended with felt pens.

The Coracle, Iona

The Speaker then passed into the Chamber. There his Chaplain has advanced to the Clerk's table, has looked at the Members and prayed for the Country.

Liverpool Echo

Mature first-growth claret and Yquem of great and outstanding vintages. Removed from the London cellar of a distinguished connoisseur, deceased now lying at Christie's.

Christie's catalogue

The city which claims to have the largest outdoor mule market in the world recently held a parade of asses led by the governor.

New York Magazine

The day after a butcher joined the staff in the Tesco supermarket in East Street, Bedminster, a series of thefts started. They were from the pockets of employees hanging in the staff rest room.

Bristol Evening Post

An 18-year-old girl accused of stealing a jar of vanishing cream has since disappeared, Huddersfield magistrates were told yesterday.

Western Mail

It's believed that they were approached by the officer when he saw them in a car which was later found acting suspiciously.

Irish Sunday Press

Sainsbury's, the London-based food giants, have taken their first steps towards building a giant super-sore in the centre of Crosby.

Crosby Herald

Fog and smog rolled over Los Angeles today, closing two airports and slowing snails down to a traffic pace.

Manchester Evening News

Councillors admitted that nude bathing was practised frequently on one of the beaches, but that burying their heads in the sand would not solve the situation.

Hobart Mercury

The council has received complaints of the dangerous condition of the road between the North Pole and East Malling and the matter is being taken up with the Kent County Council.

Kent Messenger

The Chief Fire Officer has inspected Boston Crematorium and reported to the Amenity Committee that all escape routes are adequate.

Hereford Times

Trial Judge, Lord Kincaid: 'Do I understand you correctly that you went to London and then to Amsterdam because you were murdered by Glasgow police?'

The Scotsman

A couple died when a car and a caterpillar collided at a road junction at Iyin-Ekiti, Ondo State.

Nigeria Daily Times

A printing error last week caused confusion: the price for this smartly modernised semi-detached horse in excellent position is £19,750.

Kidderminster Shuttle

You can change your life to one of complete luxury when you become the talented Receptionist in this exclusive hotel. You've been a hotel receptionist before, so you've confideddddddddddd-dddddnce in meeting people.

Reading Evening Post

She runs a small boarding house and a cottage and she was inundated with about 50 or 60 travellers from the A9 who stayed there for three Mrs Mary C——, vice-nights.

Press and Journal, Aberdeen

The assailant was described as aged between 20 and 25 years, about 5 ft 8 or 9 ins. tall, with dark hair and a moustache. He was wearing a duffle coat and had a face.

Dublin Evening Press

Female student wishes small room, with bed, breakfast and evening male.

Glasgow Evening Times

LOOK —— Free Manure.
Tons available daily.
25% off party bookings
over 20.

York and District Advertiser

The girl who lured Markham away from midnight rituals in Highgate cemetery is 26-year-old Mary Davis, a sppepeech therapist from Grimsby.

Hornsey Journal

Throwing caution to the winds, I ordered a tournedos (well done, with mixed salad and baked potatoes) and a half giraffe of wine.

Manchester Evening News

Plans to convert a Great Baddow Church to central heating have been scrapped on orders from above.

Woodham and Wickford Chronicle

Pressman gather to see Royals hung at Windsor.
Sunday Times

ANTIQUES MIGHT SOON BE
A THING OF THE PAST
Sydney Morning Herald

But even the most careful game plan can be upset by chance. It probably won't happen to you or your spouse, but what if you were to die before you were able to complete your Individual Retirement Account program? Untimely death could have a serious effect on the retirement lifestyle you've planned.
Fidelity Federal Newsletter

David Brown, of Defoe Road, Ipswich, is also charged with reckless driving in Ipswich on Henslow Road, Alan Road, Upper Cavendish Street, Tomline Road, Derby Road, Felixstowe Road, Levington Road, Nacton Road, Bishops Hill, Cavendish Street, Devonshire Road, Back Hamlet, Fore Hamlet, Fore Street, Salthouse Street, Key Street, College Street, St Peters Street, Franciscan Way, Princes Street, Ranelagh Road, Ancaster Road, Gippeswyk Avenue, Birkfield Drive, Hawthorn Drive, Kingfisher Avenue, Robin Drive and the A12 at Washbrook, Copdock, Bentley, Capel St Mary, East Bergholt, Stratford St Mary in Suffolk, and Dedham, Langham, Ardleigh, Colchester, Great Horkesley, West Bergholt, Stanway, Copford, Marks Tey and Feering in Essex. Brown was remanded in custody for seven days.
East Anglian Daily Times

Other pieces during the evening include the Piano Quartet in E Flat Major, K493, by Mozart and Walton's two pieces for lion and piano.

Sale and Altrincham Messenger

John Hacking did not believe that a man was delivering a television when he found him in his estranged wife's bedroom at midnight.

Buxton Advertiser

Wayne Denning (23) is recovering in hospital after being bitten by a German shepherd dog making a door-to-door collection for the Society for the Prevention of Cruelty to Animals.

West Australian

ERRATUM. Our ad entitled 'GIVE A BISON AS A GIFT!' published recently, should have read: Proof-brilliant field and relief presented in an attractive black case. We regret any inconvenience this may have caused. – Royal Canadian Mint.

Toronto Globe and Mail

SLAIN MAN IN LINGERIE
EATEN BY DOG

Detroit Free Press

'We appear to have a power cut here in the studio so I must apologise to listeners who may not be hearing us at the moment.'

Irish Radio announcer

ANNOUNCEMENT. This serves to inform all concerned that Mr Peter J——, who is in our employment as a Manager, will shortly be leaving the kingdom on an exit visa only. Any person having any claims against him should submit them within 7 days of this Notice appearing in the newspaper. The company will be totally irresponsible afterwards.

Saudi Arab News

Although he comes from Gloucester he's no stranger to Liverpool having been born and brought up in Manchester.

Radio Times North West

'Luther', on Sunday at 8.33 is based on John Osborne's stunning historical drama about the famous sixteenth-century cleric Albert Finney.

Pretoria News

The school is presently sited on about five acres of steep land, and has 445 children on the roll.

Lillydale & Yarra Valley Express

News of what God is doing in South Yorkshire, 'MY LEG GREW FIVE INCHES.'

The New Life

'It's a lovely plane, I have every confidence in it,' said Mr Williams. 'Why the propeller fell off I just don't know.'

Manchester Evening News

Tuesday, 2nd November, 7.45 p.m. Speaker: Mr R. Kent – 'Drugs & Drug Abuse'. There will be a Bring and Buy Stall.

A church notice in Bury St Edmond's

RED ARROWS AIR DISPLAY
IF WET, IN TOWN HALL.

R.A.C. sign in Bournemouth

CONCERTS. Ulster Orchestra. *Beethoven Night*: Mendelssohn's Elijah.

Belfast Telegraph

Mr Kass, in a wheelchair after an accident at a party, said: 'My foot is broken, but not our marriage. We are both hopping mad about the stories.'

Liverpool Daily Post

Q.   Is there any place in Palo Alto that has public shower facilities?
A.   The YMCA, 3412 Ross Road, charges 50c for a shower and 25c for a towel.
     Another idea would be to call the Stanford University Music Department, 497 3811, for a list of music students who offer lessons.

Palo Alto Weekly, California

Nowadays the death of an entertainment idol seems to have less and less effect on his or her career.

Publishers Weekly, USA

Paul Kelly of Lime Avenue, East Grinstead, was fined £15 at East Grinstead Magistrates Court on Monday for using a colour television without a silencer.

East Grinstead Observer

She had come to his house to use the phone. He had only kissed her on a Disprin for a headache he had at the time.

Southern Star

BISHOP TUTU: The ideal Christmas present for a friend.

Seek, South Africa

After the dinner, Mr Krushchev led Mrs Eisenhower by the arm down the Embassy steps, while President Eisenhower took Mrs Krushchev's ars. The Soviet Prime Minister was smiling and obviously enjoying himself.

Essex paper

MAN RECOVERING
AFTER FATAL CRASH

Limerick Weekly Echo

There was a lot of excitement and milling around, so that at last the Chairman had to call: 'I think we had better all sit down and see how we stand.'

East Anglian Magazine

The couple get their antiques through a buyer in Los Gastos who has a broker in England and accepts antiques on consignment from local persons in good condition.

Felton Valley Press, California

American electric blanket for sale, new. Owner leaving. Rosepink colour.

Advert in Sunday paper

CAPITAL PET ANIMAL HOSPITAL
Dogs called for, fleas removed
and returned to you for $5.00

Advert in Washington paper

The bride wore an ivory georgette dress with a Brussels net veil. The bridegroom wore the DSO.

South London paper

Miss Sanderton, who is only 19, has grown since last year. In patches her form is most impressive.

Essex paper

Walking sedately before the bride, came her small nephew George Stainer 3rd, carrying the ring and two little nieces of the bride.

Russel Dispatch, New Mexico

Owing to a printer's error in the 'Fairy-ring' cake recipe last week, 'two ounces castor oil' was given for 'two ounces caster sugar'. We apologise for this silly mistake.

Reveille

'The mistakes,' Cavanagh said, 'come in applying a particular modality to the wrong patient for the wrong reason at the wrong time. This is called medical judgment.'

Wisconsin State Journal

Possible side effects associated with the use of butyl – ranging from dizziness and fainting to severe headaches, loss of bowel and bladder control and cerebral haemorrhage – have drug control and consumer protection officials worried that the substance could be harmful to health.

Madison Capital Times, Wisconsin

Jelly babies depicting the Holy Family on sale in West Germany have been described by the country's Catholic bishops as 'tasteless'.

Catholic Herald

Last night a mini car swerved off the road and crashed into a lamp post in Magdalen Road, Bexhill. No casualties were reported, but communications on the 155-mile railway – only link between Addis Ababa and Djibouti – have been disrupted.

Evening News

It is proposed to re-align the road to cut out a dangerous double bed which has been the scene of numerous serious accidents in recent years.

Oxford Times

Experts know that the alcoholic process takes longer in the men, but the end reshult ies the same.

Daily Record

Pour on sufficient water to cover the giblets, boil and skim. Simmer for one hour, adding a little more water as required. Add the turkey live and cook for 20 minutes.

From a Parish magazine

Efforts to rescue three cows trapped halfway down 500-ft cliffs on the Dorset coast, near Lulworth, have been called off. A Defence Ministry statement said that they would be replaced by younger men.

West Lancashire Evening Gazette

To contact the chambermaid push the black bottom near your bed.

Notice in Verona hotel

On a local start, Christ took part in a BBC *Horizon* programme on the Eddystone Lighthouse.

Plymouth theatre programme

HOUSEHOLD AND MISCELLANEOUS FOR SALE. High Chair (converts to Electric Toaster) £8.

Royal Gazette, Bermuda

Zachowitsky came charging out like a bull at the cape. With all the coolness of an experienced matador the young forward hung on an extra second and then deftly lobbed the goalie into the empty net.

Jerusalem Post

Chulmleigh Community College: on Wednesday a Charity Concert in aid of the National Society for the Prevention of Cruelty to Children by John Clegg (international concert pianist).

North Devon Gazette

The GL auto proved capable of zero to standstill in 13.9 seconds.

Edinburgh Advertiser

Gloucester Craftsmen's Guild 1984 Spring Market, April 8. Free Admission. Free Babyshitting.

Ottawa Citizen

Strokebound holidaymakers were kept waiting six hours for the jerry. Then it was filled to capacity.

Southern Echo

A 38-year-old Northway man has again been remanded in custody charged with arson with intent to endanger the loves of his neighbours.

Gloucestershire Echo

Also rejected is an application by D.F. Austin to change a tropical fish shop at 56 View Road into a seafood restaurant.

Wakefield Express

At the heart of the ceremony Dr Harding will take the bath with his right hand on the Anglo-Saxon Gospels.

Yorkshire Evening Press

Caribbean Cruise Line require applicants experienced in pest control to train and supervise personnel aboard ship.

Glasgow Herald

The police have been combing the shanties and tent camps of itinerant people living near Broome in an effort to solve the mystery of a body found on the coastline at the weekend. Sgt Keith Kenley of the Broome police, said that there was a big floating population around the town.

The West Australian

The recipe for Scotch Oat Cakes should have read 3 cups of rolled oats and not 3 cwts.

Aylesbury Parish Magazine

Added Mrs Adams, 'When Mrs Martin told me she had been intimate with my husband I refused to give her tea.'

Daily Express

THE DAFFODIL BALL – By a misprint this ball was stated to have been organised by the National Society of Cruelty to Animals. It should, of course, have been children not animals.

Irish Independent

SIAMESE KITTENS
Very good points and eyes;
dam good pedigree.

Advert in Herts paper

Dr Arthur, who is a leading authority on this important subject, will speak on the general questions of weed control and Miss Thompson will follow with a short talk on the control of wild oats of which she has made a special study.

A committee notice

Tripoli, Saturday. The government committee for locusts is invading Libya and the country may in four months be faced with the biggest invasion on record.

Times of Cyprus

WELSH PUBLIC BODIES
GET CIRCULAR

Western Morning News

The County Surveyor proposes to put down white lines to indicate that Main Road/Windsor Road is a continuous road.

Peterborough Evening Telegraph

There were about six customers on the forecourt at the time of the raid – about 11.30 a.m. – and thieves and anybody else with information should contact police.

Southern Evening Echo

CORONER FINDS DRIVER HAD TAKEN ONLY FOUR LESSONS BEFORE HITTING CAR

Connecticut News

They kick off by investigating everything from space shuttles to tins of Britain's favourite Irishman Terry Wogan.

Bristol Evening Post

Local Planning Applications. J.S. Smith. Change of mortuary to meat processing unit, Knott Lane.

Wharfedale Observer

The Australian airline Qantas has denied one of its 747SP aircraft missed a hill on an approach to Wellington airport yesterday.

Otago Daily Times

In addition to the usual prizes, over 50 swimming certificates were presented. The school choir sank during the evening.

Oldham Chronicle

His friends will be sorry to learn that he had an operation last Wednesday and had his leg removed. All going well he should be back on his feet by the end of November.

Cobar Age, New South Wales

A few will be seated in front of the quartet in approximately a conventional concert position, while the others will have more unusual relationships with the performers.

Western Morning News

In the women's singles semi-finals of the Victorian lawn tennis championships, Miss Turner, playing her usual baseball game, confused Miss Clark.

Birmingham Evening Mail and Despatch

Joan Collins has a figure as slender as a girl's, due, she says, to living mainly on salads, 'with just one main meal a day, which is generally very lightly cooked fish or children.'

Kettering and Corby Leader

The Revd Tony Smith, rector of Wrotham, was for sale by auction this week, but withdrawn when the bidding reached £99,000.

Sevenoaks Chronicle

FOR SALE
Granite-faced Gentleman's
residence in St Saviours.

Advert in Jersey paper

When will people living in Station Cottages be rehoused, because if these houses are not soon demolished they will fall down. Rain comes down the walls like water.

Nottingham Evening Post

If two and two are put together the cat comes out of the bag.

Indian paper

If you don't have our PET/CBM catalogue phone now for your free copy. Postage free, but add 15% VAT.

Commodore Computing

Large quantities of herring and sprats have been netted by the Avock fishermen in the Inverness Town Hall during the past week.

Highland Leader

Whether shooting his best friend at sea, or in bed with his employer's wife, Ferguson remains the same bowler-hatted and inhibited Englishman.

Book review in The Observer

'We had to close the lift. An elderly person falling down the shaft is highly undesirable,' said the spokesman.

Hastings News

A man who thought a sign reading 'Fine for parking' meant it was OK to park there, has had to pay a $25 fine and $39 towing charges.

Toronto Globe and Mail

More than 5,000 computers, angry because their train was 30 minutes late, burned a police car and looted a nearby supermarket.

Sudan News Agency Bulletin

Housing compound in Riyadh for 200 families needs capable persons of strong personality has enough experience in similar position. Speaks effluent English.

Arab News

A *Globe and Mail* story about the foreign travels of the chairman of the Canadian Dairy Commission and his executive assistant was 'racist' because it linked a man and a woman, the Agriculture Minister said yesterday.

Toronto Globe and Mail

Police in Gainsborough are trying to trace a group of youths who were seen running away after a large plate of glass in the former Landers bakers shop.

Lincolnshire Echo

Mrs Ayling has let the muskrats use a room in her house as a workroom. This week they have made shell jewellery and painted Christmas boxes.

Waterbury Republican, Connecticut

Alice paused, and to hide her confusion, busied herself adjusting ornaments on the mantelpiece which needed no adjusting. Then she turned her sweet flour-like face towards him.

Short story in weekly magazine

The kick-off is at 3.15 and the teams will be found elsewhere.

Cambridge Daily News

The pigs had been sold as sound for a Barnsley man, but one died the day after and the other had to be killed to save its life.

Barnsley Chronicle

WANTED: Man to wash dishes and two waitresses.

Notice in Sydney restaurant

He told Chelmsford Crown Court: 'The law which says you must comply with an enforcement order is exactly the same law which says you must not rob or gurgle.'

Colchester Evening Echo

Miss Markham, a sociologist and police management researcher, said she decided to go to Philadelphia because there were 65 rapes a month there.

Johannesburg Star

There will be an auction in the Women's Institute Hall in aid of Church funds on Friday at 7.30 p.m. Items for the auction are urgently wanted, and we would be grateful for anything you can give, or want to get rid of. Come on the day and bring your husbands.

Stratford-on-Avon church newsletter

The footpath is a popular one and at weekends it is widely used by dog-walkers and mature lovers.

Harrogate Advertiser

'It's not like that. The noise and stench from a battery house have to be seen to be believed.'

Yorkshire Evening News

'I will not cease from Mental Fight, Nor shall my Sword sleep in my hand, Till we have built Jerusalem in England's green and pleasant land . . .' William Blake wrote these immoral words more than 150 years ago.

Bracknell News

Mrs Gladys Parkins, who runs the village shop and sub-post office at B—— has won our Glamour Competition No. 126, and will receive £200 subject to rescrutiny.

Reynolds News

A heavy pall of lust covered the upper two-thirds of Texas last night and was expected to drift south-east over the state by morning.

Yankton Press & Dispatch, S. Dakota

Domestic Help wanted; 2 adults, boy at school; modern flat; own bedroom; centrally heated foreign girl not objected to.

Advert in Hendon & Finchley Times

In the gardens lies an attractive ornamental wishing well, which the agents believe to be operational.

Leicester Mercury

At the convention, the Republicans also settled on a tactic for turning the Ferraro controversy to their own advantage by blaming Mondale and his staff for failing to screw, the vice presidential choice properly.

Arab News

The Ministry of Agriculture said: 'Everything is two to three weeks ahead in the farming world. Best lot of lambs we've seen in years and they will soon be pulling rhubarb.'

Daily Mail

Mr Farr demonstrates spinning and weaving undyed fleece into coffee and cream.

Advert in The Scotsman

Music included Love Story, Morning Has Broken, Praise My Sole the King of Heaven and the curch was decorated by Mrs Ann Brown.

Berwick Advertiser

Address and Clairvoyance Mr Benson and Mrs Dixon, Saturday 2nd June at 7.45 p.m. Cancelled due to unforeseen circumstances.

Arbroath Herald

Errors had been made by his staff, but they were only mistakes, he said.

Hull Daily Mail

If English poet John Masefield had been an Arab, his famous poem *Sea Fever* might have begun: 'I must go in a dhow to the sea again . . . '

Gulf Daily News

Anyone with brains can cook she says. Cooking should be fun, not a grind. So many people make a meal out of it.

Yorkshire Post

Nature designed the ear to clean itself. Nothing smaller than an elbow should be put into the ear to clean it.

Brampton Daily Times, Ontario

A man found in a car with his trousers down and a woman astride him was arrested for impersonating a police officer, Leeds magistrates were told yesterday.

Yorkshire Post

Wigan is suffering from an acute rise in alcoholism. For it is estimated that a staggering 2,000 people in the area have a serious drink problem.

Wigan Reporter

'I was playing the *Messiah* for about 10 minutes when she said this was not the right occasion for such music,' he went on. 'She started to make overtures to me.'

News of the World

EARS PIERCED WHILE YOU WAIT

Notice in Somerset jewellers

On Lake Ontario his wife, daughter, and twin sons threw flowers into the water along with Mr Brim's mother.

Toronto Globe and Mail

This will be a business meeting with elections for the committee together with a speaker in the form of Mr Tom Shanks, former regional analyst, who will speak on 'There is Death in the Pot.' Coffee will be available.

Law Society's Gazette

Post offices are now selling pensioners and family railcards over the counter.

Buckinghamshire Advertiser

Police said yesterday that no violence was reported during the dumping but traffic on the Catalan highway had to be rerouted temporarily into lanes free of apricots in order to avoid traffic jams.

Toronto Globe and Mail

The jet touched down in Dublin at breakfast time an hour ahead of schedule after a dense dog prevented it making a scheduled stop at Shannon on Ireland's west coast.

Journal-News, Rockland

In England, water chiefs in the parched South-West are considering a scheme to ship millions of gallons from the giant Kielder dam in Northumberland. The dam is described as 'practically full' with 44 billion galleons.

Scottish Daily Express

His interest in policing began during his national service when he served with the Royal Military Police in Gibraltar for two years. After returning to BR after his service, he applied and was Registered as a Newspaper at the Post Office.

Reading Chronicle

Rebel bus drivers sealed off Preston town centre today, blocking major Ribble bus services. For the third day running, the 70 Ribble drivers were refusing to work because of a rooster dispute.

Manchester Evening News

The item £1,631 for Centenary Entertainment will not occur again in the near future.

Report of a learned society

A resident reported she has been receiving phone calls from a male named 'Lee' for 25 years. She is tired of the calls and will change her phone number.

Monterey Bay Tribune, California

At first his appearance was unimpressive . . . It was when he was seated that one became aware of the nobility of his forehead, completed by the curve of his aquiline nose, on either side of which was a pair of shrewd, hawklike eyes.

from Deceived with Kindness *by Angelica Garnett*

SAVE $411 MICA STYLED BEDROOM

Cool almond tone, the most contemporary of styles is perfect for your home. Set includes: triple dresser, framed mirror, Queen-size headboard and one night stand.

Advert in Fort Lauderdale News

SALE: Cot, white painted, very good condition, including mattress and some baby boys, £20.

Advert in Bracknell News

The four Sundays in Advent between today and Christmas prepare us for the celebration of the first coming of Christ at Bethlehem and also for the second coming at the end of the world followed by breakfast in the J.C.R.

A Cambridge College newsletter

British Rail has a number of crossings in the pipe-line, but these will now be put on ice.

The Times

'I have several irons in the fire, but I am keeping them close to my chest.'

Quote from a football manager

Continue hanging the lengths as soon as they are pasted, butting joins precisely and wiping off any excess paste. Use a steam roller on the joins to ensure a good firm seal.

Wolverhampton Express and Star

Neil Harrison, aged 19, of Albany Street West, South Shields, was driving along the town's Mowbray Road when it swerved and hit the tree. He was freed by firemen using cutting equipment.

Sunday Sun, Newcastle

'It is quite amazing how much damage and destruction these mindless vandals can cause when they put their minds to it,' said a bitter Mr Robinson last night.

Courier and Advertiser, Fife

Dr McIntyre and his family live in a five-storey house with parents dating back to the thirteenth century.

General Practitioner

Mrs Harris told the court her husband accidentally hit her in the face with a coleslaw bowl as she held a table knife to his throat.

West Lancashire Evening Gazette

The cause of the fire at Harpers in Westover Road is still being investigated. A clairvoyant at the store said he did not predict the blaze because 'Sundays are my day off.'

Bournemouth Evening Echo

Applications are invited from applicants regardless of race, religion or sexual perversion.

Avon County Council advert

Required as soon as possible a CLASS TEACHER for a class of middle-aged children with moderate learning difficulties.

Berkshire paper

The Fifties feel i shirts, too, stay big strong for oversize drapand bright with strident jackets, often mid-thigcolours mixed in hectic length and even the morstripes, cheeks, conventional mensweageometrics and tropical manufacturers are stylin florals. Layers stay big jackets longer and loose news so why wear one shirt when you can sport If you think you're Mtwo – a collared style Cool in a bomber oover a collarless one? blouson update your.

Slough Observer

She first became interested in early music while under an undergraduate at Oxford.

BBC Proms programme

Barber Ron James called at the little cottage in Gretna Green every two months to give a short back and sides to an old and respected customer. As always bachelor Robert Hall would be in his favourite chair, riddled with woodworm and ravaged by time.

Scottish Sunday Express

One of Korea's earliest tomb epitaphs is inscribed on this tablet, but unfortunately the inscription is missing.

Korean tourism brochure

Prince Andrew's former girlfriend and the Green Shield Stamps are believed to be honeymooning 'somewhere in Britain' today after their secret wedding in a North London church.

Brighton Evening Argus

FRIDAY CLUB, Robert Bakewell School. Table tennis, darts, discos and soccer. As its name implies the club meets on Thursdays.

Loughborough Echo

The special consignments at Jacksons Ltd of Bromley this week are salmon, live lobsters, whitebait, and Marche Héroique in D flat.

Bromley District Times

We have the sad duty to inform you of the death of Marcel Giovanni, recalled to God by accident.

Paris-Normandie

The Red Cross paid for emergency care and later found a free bed for him in an institution specializing in the treatment of artcritics.

Arizona Star

The Cambridge Opera Company is no longer to be confused with the Cambridge Opera Company – or even the Cambridge Opera Company.

Cambridge Evening News

Hudson, of no fixed address, appeared before Bishop's Stortford magistrates court last Thursday and pleaded guilty to assault, threatening behaviour and criminal damage to a chocolate bar.

Bishop's Stortford Gazette

Griffithstown Junior School was designated to take 420 pupils. It now has 421 and is seriously overcrowded.

Western Mail

DEFENDANT'S SPEECH ENDS IN LONG SENTENCE

Minneapolis Tribune

People living around Stanway's new recreation area are being asked to look after the trees and shrubs placed there. They are also being asked to look out for vandals and water them if necessary.

Colchester Evening Gazette

Mr Gerald Parker of 13 Benton Road, Paignton, who died on March 7, left estate valued at £116,764 gross, £115,402 net. And his wife.

Western Morning News

Knowingly giving an accurate valuation is totally against the ethics of estate agency.

Thames Valley Property

> **INDIAN VEGETARIAN RESTAURANT**
> **Proprietor Jaya Patel cooks proprietor's mother and wife.**

Barnet Borough News

LOST: Siamese cat, very friendly, has yellow teeth. Missing from Austin Street. Could have possibly jumped into someone's car and driven off.

Standard Times, Massachusetts

The British Samaritans have tried to halt the increase in suicides from the Clifton Suspension Bridge by putting up their own sign there. The sign on the bridge asks potential suicides to telephone the Samaritans before throwing themselves off.

Western Daily Press

Stir in the tomato purée, green peppers, stock, sugar, bay leaf, and dash of nutmeg. Cover the cook in the centre of the pre-heated oven for approximately one hour.

Town Crier

Dobson was a registered alcoholic and his thoughts when he jumped into the river were to end it all. Then he remembered he could not swim and called to the policeman for help.

Exeter Express and Echo

Coun. John Black suggested royal booking for the fight to make the Welsh Office honour their commitment. He said: 'We should send a letter to the Prince of Wales as he is the ultimate in wildlife.'

North Wales Weekly News

OFFICE ASSISTANT required in central Cheadle, 4 days a week. Must be fat typist.

The Messenger, Wilmslow

Defending solicitor Mr Robert Sands suggested that Brother Garnett, a teacher, was mistaken in identifying his client as he had spoken to him through a row of runner beans.

Western Gazette

When I found them gone, I was so shocked that I washed my hair in wine, went for a stroll in the garden and drank some homemade ginger beer before going to the police.

Cape Times

If God is calling you, God will see you through. His address is: Allen Hall, 28 Beaufort Street, London SW3.

Vocational leaflet

☆ Cameron Smith – chemists, supply
Folie Perfume
This fragrance that reminds you of P
Only $39.95

Shocked by her death, Dr French commented: 'It was a tragedy. However, we cannot get neurotic over her death because I am sure it was a one-off event.'

Pulse

Swedish border police and customs and excise officers arrested six Finnish citizens on charges of smuggling Finland into Sweden last month.

Galway Sunday Tribune

DISCO. Free admission until 9.30. After 9.30, £1.00. Girls, free all night.

Eastern Evening News

It was a sort of Daniel and Goliath battle in which the stronger and bigger man always appeared to hold the mastery.

Scottish paper

THREE CLINICS ASSURE POOR
SERVICES WILL BE PROVIDED

Washington Post

The Indian Government is of the view that more than a military approach a diplomatic initiative taken by the countries of the region would pave the way for a Soviet withdrawal from Moscow.

Indian Express

Under this law it would be illegal to display in a street or other public place any written, pictorial, or other material which was held to be decent.

Greenock Telegraph

At Homewack Lodge he met his wife, Roberta, while serving her as a waiter. The romance flourished and terminated in marriage 3½ years ago.

Brooklyn Trump Village News

The Party is now debt-free. As a result of the fundraiser held in November and other fundraising efforts we now have approximately $7,000 in the Party's coiffure.

Vermont Democratic Newsletter

NOTICE

Will gentlemen taking pots of tea onto the College lawns please exercise more care. Their hot bottoms are killing the grass.

University notice

Keen educated young woman wants Agriculture or part Agriculture and Secretarial work in Blandford area. Three months farm experience, good shorthorn typist.

Advert in West Country paper

You can get an answer to any answerable question of fact or information by writing to the Question Editor:

Q. *In what book of the Bible is the proverb: 'God tempers wind to the shorn lamb'?*

A. It is on both sides of the river; Buda on one side, Pest on the other.

Q. *When and where was King Edward VII of Great Britain born?*

A. Chicago, New York, Philadelphia, Washington DC, and Baltimore, in the order named.

Q. *How much monetary gold and silver is there in the world?*

A. Approximately 1,200.

Q. *Is the claims commission of the United States and Mexico still functioning?*

A. Mixed with melted tar or pitch, it is.

Houston Press

   IN MEMORIAM

Large bathroom heater,
vanity. 26.1.72, lovingly
remembered by Vera and Jane
and Jack Wilson.

Gosford Star

The MV *Siglion* is the longest ship ever built at Laird's. Her length overall is 820 ft. The naming ceremony was performed by Mrs Doris B——, wife of Mr Simon B——, and despite her giant size she moved smoothly into the waiting waters of the Mersey.

Birkenhead News

An official not telling of the attempt to deliver the parcel was pushed through the letterbox.

Dublin Evening Press

The bride wore a gown of white satin featuring scooped neckline, elbow-length sleeves, and bell-shaped skirt, with a square train a few loose slates, and the ridge tiles silk veil fell from a satin head-band.

Southport Visitor

The chairman of the Passenger Transport Com-mittee told last night's meeting of the Plymouth City Council that he had no intention of altering the 17a bus route. 'But this does not mean we will not,' he warned.

Western Evening Herald

These are busy days for Mr Brian Smith, landlord of the Dog and Duck. Customers often follow Mr Smith out to the magpies' cage in an outbuilding, where he fills their eager beaks with milk and small pieces of bread and meat.

Leicester Mercury

It will do us within the industry no harm at all, however, to recognise that there are others who are nowhere near as hopeful about the direction in which British cheese is travelling.

Dairy Farmer

Motorists should watch out for lane closures on the A40 Western Avenue west-bound carriageway. The middle lane just west of Hanger Lane underpass is closed for 500 years.

Wycombe Star

Attractive lady would like to meet successful professional gentleman, 45-55 years for sincere and lusting relationship.

The Scotsman

Parsees perform very useful services in the port and transport business and also hold important positions as ship chandeliers.

Mag Weekly, Karachi

The Borough Council Representative, Mr John Reese, reported the date of the public inquiry about the company's application for a new whorehouse is now set for February 1.

Essex County Standard

'The facts are more consistent with the car hitting the bridge than the bridge hitting the car,' said Adrian Lenker, the president of a New Jersey engineering firm.

The Providence Journal

Have you got a secret hiding place for valuable bits and pieces? If so, write and tell me. I'll publish a selection of the best.

Tit-Bits

'According to FAA regulations, flight attendants deal with in-flight emergencies, not emergencies that occur in flight,' a spokesman said.

Rocky Mountain News

International all-round Game and Live Pigeon Shot offers FOR SALE a beautiful Double-barrel 16-bore HAMMERLESS SHOTGUN both barrels are fully choked owing to acute arthritis, owner has had to give up shooting (doctor's orders).

Advert in Manchester paper

Note to correspondent: 'Homeless'. – You have omitted to enclose your name and address. – Editor.

Jersey Evening Post

For Sale large parcel of teenage girls, various items of clothing £9.99.

Kent Evening Post

Of the 3,600 entrants this year how many could realistically expect to finish in the first three? Probably about 10.

Surrey–Hants Star

Pickles, who was fined twice, ran a big risk of losing his licence but there were exterminating circumstances in one case.

Lancs paper

The Revd Robert J—— officiated as the bride, wearing a full length crinoline dress, with a sweetheart neckline and puff sleeves, was given away by her father.

Torquay Herald Tribune

Sgt Orton, who enlisted in the Marines during his senior year of high school, had already put down roots. He and his wife, Robin, had just bought a mobile home in Jacksonville.

The Spectator, Ontario

A Manchester youth tried to avoid recognition by taking off his trousers after attempting to withdraw money with someone else's National Savings Book in Bath, city magistrates heard.

Bath & West Evening Chronicle

Two women were robbed of their handbags and one was punched in the South End district yesterday.

Boston Post

Mr Roberts went to the Deeside Enterprise Trust, a body aiming to introduce unemployment in the area and throughout the county.

Wrexham Evening Leader

To demonstrate the effectiveness of this under ideal temperature conditions, Mr Broughton showed two good-sized plants which had been only postage stamps five weeks earlier.

East Hampshire Post

Miss June Brown was a week-end guest at the Louis Scholl home. Mrs Louis Scholl was also a guest at the same home.

Ashland Times-Gazette, Ohio

CHANNEL SWIM ATTEMPT
Boston girl's arrival in Liverpool

Liverpool Echo

'But forecasting is difficult to do,' he adds, 'especially about the future.'

Infosystems

Music at MIT: presents on Sept 22 a Noon Hour Chapel Series featuring Bach's Flute Sinatras, at the MIT Chapel, free.

Somerville Journal, Massachusetts

I am also told that a gents' toilet is to be built adjacent to the sub-station. If the local inhabitants of this part of Childwall stand for this they will stand for anything.

Letter in Liverpool Echo

The number of thefts of locks, especially locks of shops, in Dessuk, Lower Egypt, has increased considerably during the last few days.

The police believe that a gang specializing in lock thefts is responsible.

Egyptian paper

Mothercare Carrycot with transporter and stand, sheets, blankets, quilt and month's M.O.T, 7,000 miles on new engine, good condition, genuine reason for sale. £525.

Grantham Journal

Sundials make a timeless garden ornament.

Surrey Mail

On the edge of the console on either side are knobs for cruise control and rear wash wipe. Storks control lights and wipers.

Loughborough and Coalville Trader

A man exposed himself to a horse after an argument with his sister-in-law, the Brisbane Magistrates Court was told yesterday.

Brisbane Courier News

BLÜTHNER pianist wanted, upright and grand.

Advert in Yorks paper

About 40 immigrants for herd-testing work, three of them women, arrived in the Atlantis yesterday morning. The three women have an agricultural background and are looking forward keenly to their new opportunities. Miss Hornimant is a B.A. (Oxen).

New Zealand paper

Newry Council refuses to buy a new piano for dancers at the town hall, because the present one smokes too much and drinks too much stout.

Sunday Express

WANTED full size violin and bow. May be antique, used or new. Top quality and condition but reasonable DISK drive – compatible with Texas instrument 99/4 home computer.

Saudi Gazette

Members heard that allowing free travel would approximately double the cost of half fare permits.

Hemel Hempstead Gazette

The 'Because We Care' ad hoc committee is disbanded due to lack of expressed interest.

Camrose County News, Alberta

Police. The body of a man was found yesterday in Ajegunie. The body had been hacked into a thousand pieces and tied in a sack. Police do not yet know if it was suicide.

Nigerian National Concord

As family and guests posed for wedding photographs outside Norwich register office, a gust of wind blew away Dave's mother-in-law, Mr June Wilson's £30 hat.

Liverpool Echo

Regulars at the Tudor Hotel raised £140 for cancer research from a raffle of one of their customers.

Malvern Gazette and Ledbury Reporter

Work is nearing completion on the new workshop which will provide facilities for woodwork, furniture repairs, soft toy making, and other useful work, while the activities room has recently had a dark room added for those wanting to learn about philosophy.

Harlow News

Tottenham, still without the two injured players, fell behind after just three minutes when Slack Marking allowed David Moss to shoot Luton ahead.

Khaleej Times

The crowd of 15,630 was disappointingly low on an afternoon when Town boss Jameson was in pain after having injections for a trapped nerve in the neck.

East Anglian Daily Times

Former Labour party leader Michael Foot may visit Sheffield in a bid to solve the growing problem of the Indian state of Kashmir.

Sheffield Star

Darts (P2) Later learned officers attacked with darts were carrying picket, crushed by crows, from scene on police protection shield. Injured officer has two puncture wounds in check.

Birmingham Evening Mail

The incident happened at 2.10 a.m. when the sister was going to the ladies toilet at the burns unit. The toilet sprang out and slashed her arm with a knife.

St Helen's Star

A Gwent diver who stole coins and treasure from the Mary Rose has been a 'nervous wreck' since his arrest, a London court heard.

South Wales Argus

The new lizard, 21 in. long, is said at the Zoo to be settling down well. It is described by a keeper as being as lively as the cricketers that are part of its favourite diet.

Lincolnshire Echo

MEAT IN BEEF SAUSAGES
Prestatyn butcher fined £5

Liverpool Echo

Blend sugar, flour and salt. Add egg and milk, cook until creamy in double boiler. Stir frequently. Add rest of ingredients. Mix well and serve chilled. Funeral services will be held Thursday afternoon at two o'clock.

Reedsburg Post

Kuwait Cultural Centre will take part in a rhubarb and violin concert at the Sadu House on March 18.

Arab Times

Chaos hit the Birmingham southbound section of the M6 today after a lorry shed its trailer load of pig carcases, causing tailbacks of more than three miles.

Birmingham Evening Mail

ARIES (March 21-April 19): Get an early tart today to complete weekend chores.

Mexico City News

Dr Charles said they had removed three bullets from Mrs Morris, one from each leg.

The Scotsman

Miss Turner has set up a campaign against incestuous relationships at the house in Twyford Road where she loves with her parents.

Enfield Gazette

Belcoo police seized twenty cattle and thirty small pigs on suspicion of having been smuggled, assisted by Miss K. McDermott (violin) and Mrs P. O'Malley (percussion and effects).

Fermanagh Herald

After cooking a pie from a can of stewed steak a family sat down to eat it. A daughter found a stud-type earring in her portion and her father found a stud earring in his piece. Unfortunately the two did not match.

Herts Advertiser

Over 50 children took advantage of the mobile clinic and were examined for tuberculosis and other diseases which the clinic offered free of charge.

Boston News

'I find streaking morally wrong. If the good Lord had intended us to run around with no clothes on I'm sure we would all have been born naked.'

Attributed to a Midland councillor

She is Petty Officer Laura Brown, aged 17, of Folkestone, and she will sail from Portsmouth on May 28 and be at sea until June 10. She will be a member of the crew compromising girls from all over the country.

Local paper

A Wallasey man was working on an electricity pylon when it was struck by lightning. He escaped by a hare's breath.

Wallasey paper

There's no bad form about tea drinking (although slurping it from the saucer is somewhat *de rigueur*).

Quest/77

The school will emphasise the basic sciences, however, he said. 'Compassion and sympathy cannot compensate for scientific ignorance. You have to have both.'

San Juan Star, Puerto Rico

Versatile casual trouser suit by Elida. The jacket has single button cuffs, decorative breast pocket flaps, an optional belt and curved side vents. The trousers are slightly flared and fall straight to the ground.

Gloucestershire & Avon Life

With this new location we are able to distribute more data much faster. Our goal is to have your printed material in your mailbox within 30 minutes after completion of your execution.

U.S. House of Representatives newsletter

At International House, 370 Chestnut Street, the weekend of Feb 4-5, the Ethnic Folklife Festival will have as focus THE FORKLIFT TRADITIONS of the Balkan and Chinese communities.

Cherry Hill Lakes Shopper's Guide

Through co-operative efforts of three fire departments the home of Mike Lewis, who lives near Harbin's Store, was almost completely destroyed on Saturday afternoon.

Louisville Lafayette County Democrat

Correction
Because of a telephone mishearing the Prime Minister was incorrectly quoted in later editions of *The Times* yesterday. His remark should have read, 'You expect to pay for going to the Louvre.'

The Times

Practise the art of deep breathing. After the morning bath take a deep breath, retain it as long as possible, then slowly expire.

Home Chat

She was quizzing people outside the Whitgift Centre about their knowledge of nuclear terminology, when she says six policemen and a dog asked her to move on.

Croydon News

Wolverhampton B.C.: Adventure Play Leader. See under Burial and Cremation.

Opportunities Magazine

Two thousand graves are to be dug up as part of a kiss of life scheme for West Ham cemetery.

Stratford and Newham Express

Hamster for sale, complete with starter unit and wheel, £5 only.

Watford Weekend Plus

Communicate direct to Transport Officer in case of accidents. As members give their services voluntarily, reasonable notice should be given – 24 hours whenever possible.

Gloucester paper

Bethel Chapel. The Ladies Friendly Hour was hell on Thursday, when Mrs Jones, of Liverpool, was the speaker.

Westmorland Gazette

In association with the Merton Council of Churches, the united choirs, interdenominational and Wilton orchestra will give Bach's 'The Passion of Our Lord According to St Mansel Road, Wimbledon.'

Wimbledon News

Mr Leonard Holder served as a second-lieutenant in the Machine Gun Corps in the First World War, which perhaps confirmed his fondness of music and cricket.

Stoke-on-Trent Evening Sentinel

Pupils at Snape Hill Road Junior and Infants School, Darfield, were given an illustrated slide show on birds by a representative of the Royal Society for the Prevention of Birds.

Barnsley Star

NEW MILTON, Hants. – Between sea and New Forest. Comfortably furnished detached MOUSE TO LET.

Advert in Church Times

After the wettest June ever recorded in the area, water-borne pests such as gnats and midges are breeding like flies.

Newcastle Advertiser

McCarthys Ltd is to close its Edinburgh depot at the end of September. A spokesman said on August 3: 'We are contracting into a larger unit.'

Pharmaceutical Journal

I HAVE seen Jesus Christ, so can you! Send $3.00 (handling fee) to Direct Path, Box 5611.

National Examiner

Supt. John Robins said the defendant collided with an oncoming vehicle. At the time the defendant was completely on his incorrect side of the road, but would have been on his correct side had he been in Germany.

Irish Press

Fisherman cheats death by drowning.

South China Morning Post

Mary was one of the policewomen who made the Queen's visit to open the new Chapter House in St Albans on July 8 a huge and happy success. She was pictured entering into the carnival atmosphere carrying armfuls of flowers and with a huge smile on her foot.

Watford Evening Echo

A 21-year-old butcher was unfairly dismissed when he was given the chop, a Gloucester Industrial Tribunal has decided.

Gloucestershire Echo

American sailor James Edwards talked today about his fight for life in six-metre seas. 'I thought I was going to bite the dust,' he said.

Perth Daily News

Firearms (11 weeks) Course. It is hoped to include both theoretical and practical aspects of firearms usage. Target: 20 students.

Late Extra, Bradford

All competitors will be required to run with their personal particulars in a plastic bag.

Zimbabwe Sunday Mail

The sex-shop provisions of the Local Government Bill were tightened by the Lords last night to include hovercraft.

Sheffield Morning Telegraph

If toads are having problems with traffic there are a variety of ways to help them including road signs.

Natural World

Six dresses, two blouses, two skirts and two blue nighties have been stolen from the men's dressing room at Trinity and All Saints' Colleges at Horsforth, Leeds.

Yorkshire Evening Post

Cllr Adams explained that the new scheme was not inferior, only not as good as the first.

Thame Gazette

At Mwnt, the warm weather brought the shoals of mackerel close inshore, with schools of porpoises following them. It was the same story in the mountains.

Cambrian News

If you ask the average American for a detailed description of the bed he sleeps in, he will probably be unable to oblige you. He can precisely visualise his cravats, his overcoats, his golf clubs, or his automobile, but his bed and furniture are merely nebulous conveniences in his mind. And the same thing is true of his wife.

Fortune

There was no question of the aircraft having been sabotaged, according to the spokesman who said it was a technical fault. There was no question of an enquiry other than that people would be asking exactly what happened.

Cork Examiner

Five Labradors trained to sniff out contraband were arrested for being drunk and incapable when 330 cases of whisky were smashed as a lorry over-turned in Somerset.

Commercial Motor

It is embarrassing to observe the way in which the mineworkers' president is behaving. Mr Scargill's brains appear to have gone to his head.

Wolverhampton Express and Star

It was such a success that the organisers are not thinking of making it an annual event.

Hatfield Review

Mr and Mrs Horace Cresswell, of Tennessee, are seeing their loved ones here. Dr C.H. Workman removed Mr Cresswell's tonsils and they are now with his sister, Mrs Palmer.

Greenwood Journal, South Carolina

AUTOMATIC 1300 Austin, K reg, long M.O.T., taxed Jan, radio, woman, £300.

Richmond and Twickenham Guardian

Watford's number two Mastermind goes into Westminster Hospital on Thursday for major heart surgery. He said this week: 'They tell me that after the operation I shall even be able to play tennis. That's strange, because I don't play tennis.'

Watford Observer

If a litter bin is provided at the lay-by on the A6 in Shardlow, it will attract rubbish, fears the parish council.

Long Eaton Advertiser

Uniforms with medals will be worn at the reception of General Allan Brewster, Tuesday evening. Trousers optional.

Norfolk News, Virginia

Three police officers our reporter spoke to in the town said that police officers generally were in favour of hanging, including themselves.

Bournemouth Evening Echo

From July all buses from Loughton Garage will be single deckers, explained Mr Barnes. This would keep down the overheads.

West Essex Gazette

The Ashford Branch of the Men of Kent and Kentish Men held its Annual General Meeting recently. Officers elected were President Miss Mary Green, Chairman Miss Wanda Marks, Secretary Mrs Joan Knight, Social Secretary Miss Jean Robinson, and Publicity officer Miss Wanda Marks.

Ashford Advertiser

On the way out to the Middle East, he recalls, they travelled via the Cape on the Queen Mary, with 10,000 troops and 16 officers sharing a two-berth cabin.

Canberra Standard

Cypriot coffee is bitter, black and cinnamony. Not everybody's cup of tea.

Destination India

Nothing could be further from the truth, apart from the fact that world-wide statistics have failed to prove that hanging is an effective detergent.

Kingston and Surrey Guardian

SERVICE HAND. Mon-Fri. 10.30-3.30. £7 to serve waitresses from the hot plate. Tel: MIN 9999.

Evening Standard

Mr Steward had shrapnel injuries to both eyes, but took part in the withdrawal from Blackpool, walking for three days through dense jungle and over high hill ranges in the monsoon.

Leicester Mercury

Station Inspector Donald Roberts said he was busy in his office when he heard a car travelling at high speed and then people screaming on the platform. Outside he saw a new car with all four of the wheels in the air and the axles resting on the railway lines. He did not like it because last year his station took the award for the neatest station in the area.

Durban Daily News

As part of a project on infant care, students have to simulate parenthood by taking care of a hard-boiled egg for a week.

Nursing paper

Mai Thai Finn is one of the students in the programme and was in the centre of the photo. We incorrectly listed her name as one of the items on the menu.

Auckland Star

'I applied in a local magazine for help in raising money for her to buy a wheelchair and the response was tremendous. Sadly she died just before we were able to buy the wheelchair, but we bought it in memory of her.'

Leamington Spa Courier

What he describes as a significant finding is that breast-fed babies consult their doctors less often than bottle-fed babies.

Glasgow Herald

FREE
Small flat wife to manage launderette

Advert in Evening Standard

The same was experienced by Mr and Mrs Pratt of the Kings Arms. They said their trade had improved recently renovated the old bar and lounge, and Mrs Pratt considerably.

Oxford Times

To prevent your eyes watering when slicing onions dip them into boiling water for a few seconds.

Sunday News, New Zealand

This is the story of four men and a woman, spanning the years from the height of the war to the present day. It takes in an underwear hunt.

Hemel Hempstead Gazette

8.30 p.m. Free CBC concert.
Mary Morrison, soprano
Viola da Gamba, harpsichord

Toronto Citizen

Midnight mass will be celebrated in the Milandes chapel at 9 o'clock on Tuesday morning.

Sud-Ouest

Arrested by inspectors in Saint-Germain-des-Prés, he was recognised as having caused the fatal accident of which he had been the victim in August last year.

Nouveau-Nord

Sir, the first time I heard the cuckoo was on April 12th. Flying overhead from the garden, my husband heard it before that date.

Western Gazette

Brown said there was no danger to the animals. Each pig will be strapped into a custom-made harness and attached to a parachute with a human sky-diver.

'If the pig does, the skydiver dies,' said Brown. 'We're very safety conscious.'

Canadian Sunday Sun

Mr Blore, who died on August 20, aged 66, had promised her lifetime support and a home in return for devoting all of her time to him. She said that for 12 years preceding his death she kept her part of the promise, except for brief periods when she was married to three other men.

New Zealand Herald

More than 2,000 people under 65 died each year in the Oxford region due to heart disease. For one in five, the first sign that they are suffering from heart disease is sudden death.

Abingdon Herald

They gave the go-ahead this week to take a positive lead in felling and treating all dead elms seriously affected by the disease on their own property and to take steps to ensure that owners of dead or dying trees also be felled and destroyed.

Musselburgh News

The duo of Jan Wentworth as Rosalie and Pat Moore as the domineering Madame Rosepetal went so well that one moment one could hear a pin drop, at another there was not a dry seat in the auditorium.

Sunday Times of Zambia

Then one of the newer Labour MPs rushed across the floor to shake a clenched fish in the Prime Minister's face.

Western Mail

A salvo of shots was fired as six burglars played the Last Post.

Ilford Recorder

If it wasn't for those bright sparks who discovered electricity in what is so aptly called the dim and distant past, we'd be watching television by candlelight every night of the week.

Manchester Evening News and Chronicle

A doctor has compiled a list of poisons which children may drink at home.

Ottawa Journal

All he asked was a fireside chair and a couple of good boobs.

Cape Times

When the police arrived at the accident they smelled of alcohol and he was taken to Bury Police Station.

Bury Times

At 10.15 an employee of Gourock Town Council lit the bonfire and in seconds it was a flaming beacon. It was midnight before the last of the burning members were extinguished.

Greenock Telegraph

Sister Gillian's 'bust clinic' referred to last month was, of course, a 'busy clinic'.

Berkshire parish magazine

Happy sequel to boy and girl courtship
FLU DELAYS WEDDING
Headlines in Nebraska paper

The seats in the vicinity of the bandstand are for the use of ladies. Gentlemen should make use of them only after the former are seated.

Notice in Ohio park

John Benson, who was run down·at the same time, died of his injuries. Last night his temperature declined somewhat.

Wilkes-Barre Record

For several weeks this difference has only been visible to those who are closing their eyes to a tragic reality.

Echo-Liberté

The five who returned today consisted of three Polish Alpinists who climbed back down to Chamonix, and two Swiss climbers who arrived safely at the Téléférique terminal of Montenvers, below the glacier, the Merde Glace.

Daily Telegraph

After the electricity board failed to read her meter for ten quarter periods, Mrs Barrett was landed with a huge bull.

Newcastle Evening Chronicle

Joe Stanhope, of Streator, has just received a letter from his wife in Italy telling of the birth of a son. Joe immediately set the boys up to drinks, and stated that he had not seen his wife for five years.

Washburn Leader, Illinois

FOR SALE, motor bike,
suit 34 bust.

Advert in South London paper

Two men were arrested on Thursday for the theft
of a cartload of girdles. If convicted, the FBI says,
they face a ten-year stretch.

Philadelphia Inquirer

The defence claim that the words mhm mh mh h
hm were no libel and that the words in their natural
and ordinary signification were true in substance
and in fact.

Irish Independent

Staffordshire Education Committee.
Required for February:
MISTRESS FOR PIANIST

Advert in Wolverhampton Express and Star

The Minister warned that violent revolution in
South Africa could only be avoided if racial injustice
was stamped out there with a 38 in. telescope.

Swindon Evening Advertiser

He was Chairman of Berwickshire Hunt Committee from December 1962. He rode regularly to
hounds until his death would not allow him to do so.

Berwickshire News

Among the crowd of guests who stood on Bristol dockside on a cold day this spring to watch Lord Beswick, the chairman of British Aerospace, arrive by toad to open the city's new Industrial Museum, there must have been quite a number who were less than convinced of the future popularity of the venture.

Gloucestershire and Avon Life

But the Ministry of Defence now says it will maintain neutrality though agreeing to supply both sides with arms.

Lloyd's List

Mr and Mrs William Snyder of 430 Thurston Avenue wish to announce the birth of a six and one-half pound baby daughter on Wednesday noon. The youngster has been called North Prospect Street.

Sentinel Tribune, Oregon

SANDWICH RECIPE – Butter slices of bread and on each lay a thin slice of American cheese the corps as well as officers of our own military forces, in uniform, making the scene scarcely second in brilliance to the White House reception, seasoning it with salt, mustard, paprika and a dash of cayenne.

San Diego Union

For his contribution to community relations, Constable Alan Barr was commended, as were Constables George Carter and Neil Markham, responsible for numerous robberies on elderly women.

Liverpool Daily Post

Police have not released the name of the Mini driver, who was unhurt. The Mini was driven by Gladys Brett of Halesowen, who was not hurt.

Wolverhampton Express and Star

Newsletter 286 contained an item describing the renovations on the main floor of the Administrative Building. 'Wall has been removed' should, of course, have read 'A wall has been removed'. We apologise to Dr Wall, whose office is in this area, for any inconvenience he may have experienced as a result of this error.

University of Manitoba Faculty newsletter

Builder's labrador required. Able to drive an advantage though not essential.

Advert in Yorkshire Evening Press

Bound, gagged and trussed up nude in a denim bag, with plugs in her ears and tape over her eyes, Cleveland teacher Linda Barnett told yesterday how she was kidnapped to Florida, not knowing where she was going or why.

Cleveland Plain Dealer

Black panther leader Huey Newton, terming a 1974 murder charge 'strictly a fabrication', said yesterday he will testify at his trial on charges of killing a prostitute against his lawyer's advice.

Cleveland Plain Dealer

Mr Roberts said he could not give a firm answer on the hospital's future. He was watched by nurses from the hospital in the Stranglers' Gallery.

Derby Evening Telegraph

A judge has ordered formal not guilty verdicts at Bristol Crown Court in the case of two British Rail stewards accused of going equipped for theft with a piece of cheese.

Bristol Evening Post

One witness told the commissioners that she had seen sexual intercourse taking place between two parked cars in front of her house.

The Press (Atlantic City)

Teller Stuns Man
With Stolen Check

Philadelphia Evening Bulletin

Owners of all dogs in the city of Metropolis are required to be on a chain or in a fenced-in area.

Metropolis Planet, Illinois

Mrs Enid Patterson said: 'We have to get this thrashed out once and for all. I don't want to see the bus station end up as a white elephant around this town's neck.'

Dartmouth Chronicle

MAN EATING PIRANHA
MISTAKENLY SOLD AS PET FISH

The Milwaukee Journal

Sultan had beaten a Bradford goldsmith, leaving him self-conscious.

Leamington & District Morning News

THOUGHT FOR THE DAY . . . So they hurried off and found Harry and the baby lying in the manger – Luke, chapter 2, verse 16.

Essex Chronicle

Zambia produced 609,294 tonnes of finished steel to maintain its position as the fifth largest producer of copper in the world.

Commonwealth

The survey found there was a general tendency to see AIDS as a threat to homosexuals and drug users. This was despite other research that showed homosexuals accounted for 80 per cent of those engaged in high-rise behaviour.

Westside Express, Brisbane

All Futura Books are available at your bookshop or
newsagent, or can be ordered from the following address:
Futura Books, Cash Sales Department,
P.O. Box 11, Falmouth, Cornwall TR10 9EN.

Please send cheque or postal order (no currency), and
allow 60p for postage and packing for the first book
plus 25p for the second book and 15p for each additional
book ordered up to a maximum charge of £1.90 in U.K.

B.F.P.O. customers please allow 60p for
the first book, 25p for the second book plus 15p per
copy for the next 7 books, thereafter 9p per book

Overseas customers, including Eire, please allow £1.25
for postage and packing for the first book, 75p for the
second book and 28p for each subsequent title ordered.